Published by Bound Books in 2022.
Bound Books is an imprint of Wildling Books Ltd.

Printed in China by 1010 Printing International Limited.

www.wildlingbooks.com

INTUITION

It holds the answers you seek

Intuition is our ability to access knowledge from within us, without help from the outside world. Often when no one knows the 'right' thing to do, your inner compass ensures you steer your course in a certain way, or signals to you a sure 'yes' or 'no' through an internal energy.

Intuition is your superpower. It holds an immense creative energy that we can tap into to help us give meaning to our life and make a positive difference in this world. It can provide us with solutions when we know how to access the limitless knowledge that lies within us all.

Use an intuition notebook to explore why things have come up for you. It can be a place where you can make notes, record signs that you notice and write about dreams that you have. By writing things down, you're giving yourself a chance to delve deeper into the meaning of these things and strengthen your connection with your intuition.

Do you sense a particular message coming through or do you have a gut feeling about something? Write it all down. It doesn't need to make sense. It could be just words, questions, or feelings you are experiencing –whatever it is, throw it all down on paper.

After a period of time, you may be able to look at these notes and see them come together into a coherent message.

Record your dreams

Keep this notebook and a pen beside your bed, so that when you wake, you can write down anything you remember about the dreams you've had. This will help you to work out what your subconscious mind is pondering while you sleep. Sometimes you may just remember small things, other times you may remember more lengthy scenes. Jot down whatever you recall, and over time, these notes may start making more sense to you.

To understand your purpose or find more meaning, listen to the whispers from your soul and look for the clues that the universe scatters before you.

Everything is connected. Everything is of value. You can find a deeper meaning everywhere. Start looking and be open to the signs around you.

Everyone is the centre of their own universe.

Our intuition is our inner compass,
there to gently guide us along our path.

By tapping into that which you already know, you will begin to trust yourself wholly, as the magnificent being you are.

It’s time to start noticing, to start listening to that which has no words but moves us by using energy.

Your intuition is your link to the collective consciousness, to your spirituality, your God or gods, to the light and love shining within you, to the all-knowing wisdom.

Live your life in a state of wonder
and awe at the true blessing
it is to be alive in this moment.

The more you use your intuition, the easier it becomes for you to dial into it through feelings, dreams, smells, sounds, synchronicities, signs and symbols.